Selected Writings
of Shoghi Effendi

Selected Writings of Shoghi Effendi

Bahá'í Publishing Trust
Wilmette, Illinois 60091

ISBN 0-87743-079-9

Printed in United States of America

Contents

Excerpts from the Will and Testament
of 'Abdu'l-Bahá

O my loving friends! After the passing away of this wronged one, it is incumbent upon the Aghsán (Branches), the Afnán (Twigs) of the Sacred Lote-Tree, the Hands (pillars) of the Cause of God and the loved ones of the Abhá Beauty to turn unto Shoghi Effendi—the youthful branch branched from the two hallowed and sacred Lote-Trees and the fruit grown from the union of the two offshoots of the Tree of Holiness,—as he is the sign of God, the chosen branch, the guardian of the Cause of God, he unto whom all the Aghsán, the Afnán, the Hands of the Cause of God and His loved ones must turn. He is the expounder of the words of God. . . .

The sacred and youthful branch, the guardian of the Cause of God as well as the Universal House of Justice, to be universally elected and established, are both under the care and protection of the Abhá Beauty, under the shelter and unerring guidance of His Holiness, the Exalted One (may my life be offered up for them both). . . .

A Summary

1. The Revelation proclaimed by Bahá'u'lláh, His followers believe, is divine in origin, all-embracing in scope, broad in its outlook, scientific in its method, humanitarian in its principles and dynamic in the influence it exerts on the hearts and minds of men. The mission of the Founder of their Faith, they conceive it to be to proclaim that religious truth is not absolute but relative, that Divine Revelation is continuous and progressive, that the Founders of all past religions, though different in the non-essential aspects of their teachings, *"abide in the same Tabernacle, soar in the same heaven, are seated upon the same throne, utter the same speech and proclaim the same Faith."* His Cause, they have already demonstrated, stands identified with, and revolves around, the principle of the organic unity of mankind as representing the consummation of the whole process of human evolution. This final stage in this stupendous evolution, they assert, is not only necessary but inevitable, that it is gradually approaching, and that nothing short of the celestial potency with which a divinely ordained Message can claim to be endowed can succeed in establishing it.

The Bahá'í Faith recognizes the unity of God and of His Prophets, upholds the principle of an unfettered search after truth, condemns all forms of superstition and prejudice, teaches that the fundamental purpose of religion is to promote concord and harmony, that it must go hand-in-hand with science, and that it constitutes the sole and ultimate basis of a peaceful, an ordered and progressive society. It inculcates the principle of equal opportunity, rights and privileges for both sexes, advocates compulsory education, abolishes extremes of poverty and wealth, exalts work performed in the spirit of service to the rank of worship, recommends the adoption of an auxiliary international language, and provides the necessary agencies for the establishment and safeguarding of a permanent and universal peace.

Born about the middle of the nineteenth century in darkest Persia, assailed from its infancy by the forces of religious fanaticism, the Faith has, notwithstanding the martyrdom of its Forerunner, the repeated banishments of its Founder, the almost life-long imprisonment of its chief Promoter and the cruel death of no less than twenty thousand of its devoted followers, succeeded in diffusing quietly and steadily its spirit throughout both the East and the West, . . . and has recently obtained from the ecclesiastical and civil authorities in various lands written affirmations that recognize its independent religious status.

The Forerunner of the Faith was Mírzá 'Alí-Muḥammad of Shíráz, known as the Báb (The Gate) Who proclaimed on May 23, 1844, His twofold mission as an independent Manifestation of God and Herald of One greater than Himself, Who would inaugurate a new and unprecedented era in the religious history of mankind. On His early life, His sufferings, the heroism of His disciples, and the circumstances of His tragic martyrdom I need not dwell, as the record of His saintly life is minutely set forth in *The Dawn-Breakers: Nabíl's Narrative of the Early Days of the Bahá'í Faith*. Suffice it to say that at the early age of thirty-one the Báb was publicly martyred by a military firing squad at Tabríz, Persia, on July 9, 1850. On the evening of that same day His mangled body was removed from the courtyard of the barracks to the edge of the moat outside the gate of the city whence it was carried by His fervent disciples to Ṭihrán. There it remained concealed until such time as its transfer to the Holy Land was made possible. Faced by almost insuperable difficulties and facing the gravest dangers a band of His disciples, acting under the instructions of 'Abdu'l-Bahá succeeded in transporting overland the casket containing His remains to Haifa. In 1909, 'Abdu'l-Bahá with his own hands and in the presence of the assembled representatives of various Bahá'í communities deposited those remains within the vault of the Mausoleum he himself had erected for the Báb. Ever since that time countless followers of the Bahá'í Faith have made the pilgrimage to this sacred spot, a spot which ever since 1921 has been further sanctified by the burial of 'Abdu'l-Bahá in an adjoining vault.

The Founder of the Faith was Bahá'u'lláh (Glory of God), Whose advent the Báb had foretold. He declared His mission in 1863 while an exile in Baghdád. He subsequently formulated the principles of that new and divine civilization which by His advent He claimed to have inaugurated. He too was bitterly opposed, was stripped of His property and rights, was exiled to 'Iráq, to Constantinople and Adrianople, and was eventually incarcerated in the penal colony of 'Akká where He passed away in 1892 in His seventy-fifth year. His remains are laid to rest in the Shrine at Bahjí, north of 'Akká.

The authorized Interpreter and Exemplar of Bahá'u'lláh's teachings was His eldest son 'Abdu'l-Bahá (Servant of Bahá) who was appointed by his Father as the Center to whom all Bahá'ís should turn for instruction and guidance. 'Abdu'l-Bahá ever since his childhood was the closest companion of his Father, and shared all His sorrows and sufferings. He remained a prisoner until 1908, when the old régime in Turkey was overthrown and all religious and political prisoners throughout the empire were liberated. After that he continued to make his home in Palestine but undertook extensive teaching tours in Egypt, Europe and America, being ceaselessly engaged in explaining and exemplifying the principles of his Father's Faith and in inspiring and directing the activities of his friends and followers throughout the world. He passed away in 1921 in Haifa, Palestine, and, as already stated, was buried in a vault contiguous to that of the Báb on Mount Carmel.

Divine Revelation Is Progressive

2. The Revelation, of which Bahá'u'lláh is the source and center, abrogates none of the religions that have preceded it, nor does it attempt, in the slightest degree, to distort their features or to belittle their value. It disclaims any intention of dwarfing any of the Prophets of the past, or of whittling down the eternal verity of their teachings. It can, in no wise, conflict with the spirit that animates their claims, nor does it seek to undermine the basis of any man's allegiance to their cause. Its declared, its primary purpose is to enable every adherent of these Faiths to obtain a fuller understanding of the religion with which he stands identified, and to acquire a clearer apprehension of its purpose. It is neither eclectic in the presentation of its truths, nor arrogant in the affirmation of its claims. Its teachings revolve around the fundamental principle that religious truth is not absolute but relative, that Divine Revelation is progressive, not final. Unequivocally and without the least reservation it proclaims all established religions to be divine in origin, identical in their aims, complementary in their functions, continuous in their purpose, indispensable in their value to mankind.

"All the Prophets of God," asserts Bahá'u'lláh in the Kitáb-i-Íqán, *"abide in the same tabernacle, soar in the same heaven, are seated upon the same throne, utter the same speech, and proclaim the same Faith."* From the *"beginning that hath no beginning,"* these Exponents of the Unity of God and Channels of His incessant utterance have shed the light of the invisible Beauty upon mankind, and will continue, to the *"end that hath no end,"* to vouchsafe fresh revelations of His might and additional experiences of His inconceivable glory. To contend that any particular religion is final, that *"all Revelation is ended, that the portals of Divine mercy are closed, that from the dayfsprings of eternal holi-*

ness no sun shall rise again, that the ocean of everlasting bounty is forever stilled, and that out of the Tabernacle of ancient glory the Messengers of God have ceased to be made manifest" would indeed be nothing less than sheer blasphemy.

"They differ," explains Bahá'u'lláh in that same epistle, *"only in the intensity of their revelation and the comparative potency of their light."* And this, not by reason of any inherent incapacity of any one of them to reveal in a fuller measure the glory of the Message with which He has been entrusted, but rather because of the immaturity and unpreparedness of the age He lived in to apprehend and absorb the full potentialities latent in that Faith.

3. If the light that is now streaming forth upon an increasingly responsive humanity with a radiance that bids fair to eclipse the splendor of such triumphs as the forces of religion have achieved in days past; if the signs and tokens which proclaimed its advent have been, in many respects, unique in the annals of past Revelations; if its votaries have evinced traits and qualities unexampled in the spiritual history of mankind; these should be attributed not to a superior merit which the Faith of Bahá'u'lláh, as a Revelation isolated and alien from any previous Dispensation, might possess, but rather should be viewed and explained as the inevitable outcome of the forces that have made of this present age an age infinitely more advanced, more receptive, and more insistent to receive an ampler measure of Divine Guidance than has hitherto been vouchsafed to mankind.

. . . Who, contemplating the helplessness, the fears and miseries of humanity in this day, can any longer question the necessity for a fresh revelation of the quickening power of God's redemptive love and guidance? Who, witnessing on one hand the stupendous advance achieved in the realm of human knowledge, of power, of skill and inventiveness, and viewing on the other the unprecedented character of the sufferings that afflict, and the dangers that beset, present-day society, can be so blind as to doubt that the hour has at last struck for the advent of a new Revelation, for a re-statement of the Divine Purpose, and for the consequent revival of those spiritual forces that have, at fixed intervals, rehabilitated the fortunes of human society? Does not the very operation of the world-unifying forces that are at work in this age necessitate that He Who is the Bearer of the Message of God in this day should not only reaffirm that self-same exalted standard of individual conduct inculcated by the Prophets gone before Him, but embody in His appeal, to all governments and peoples, the essentials of that social code, that Divine Economy, which must guide humanity's concerted efforts in establishing that all-embracing federation which is to signalize the advent of the Kingdom of God on this earth?

4. The Faith of Bahá'u'lláh should indeed be regarded, if we wish to be faithful to the tremendous implications of its message, as the culmination of a cycle, the final stage in a series of successive, of preliminary and progressive revelations. These, beginning with Adam and ending with the Báb, have paved the way and anticipated with an ever-increasing emphasis the advent of that Day of Days in which He Who is the Promise of All Ages should be made manifest.

To this truth the utterances of Bahá'u'lláh abundantly testify. A mere reference to the claims which, in vehement language and with compelling power, He Himself has repeatedly advanced cannot but fully demonstrate the character of the Revelation of which He was the chosen bearer. To the words that have streamed from His pen—the fountainhead of so impetuous a Revelation—we should, therefore, direct our attention if we wish to obtain a clearer understanding of its importance and meaning. Whether in His assertion of the unprecedented claim He has advanced, or in His allusions to the mysterious forces He has released, whether in such passages as extol the glories of His long-awaited Day, or magnify the station which they who have recognized its hidden virtues will attain, Bahá'u'lláh and, to an almost equal extent, the Báb and 'Abdu'l-Bahá, have bequeathed to posterity mines of such inestimable wealth as none of us who belong to this generation can befittingly estimate. Such testimonies bearing on this theme are impregnated with such power and reveal such beauty as only those who are versed in the languages in which they were originally revealed can claim to have sufficiently appreciated. So numerous are these testimonies that a whole volume would be required to be written in order to compile the most outstanding among them. All I can venture to attempt at present is to share with you only such passages as I have been able to glean from His voluminous writings.

"*I testify before God,*" proclaims Bahá'u'lláh, "*to the greatness, the inconceivable greatness of this Revelation. Again and again have We in most of Our Tablets borne witness to this truth, that mankind may be roused from its heedlessness.*" "*In this most mighty Revelation,*" He unequivocally announces, "*all the Dispensations of the past have attained their highest, their final consummation.*" "*That which hath been made manifest in this preëminent, this most exalted Revelation, stands unparalleled in the annals of the past, nor will future ages witness its like.*" "*He it is,*" referring to Himself He further proclaims, "*Who in the Old Testament hath been named Jehovah, Who in the Gospel hath been designated as the Spirit of Truth, and in the Qur'án acclaimed as the Great Announcement.*" "*But for Him no Divine Messenger would have been invested with the robe of prophethood, nor would any of the sacred scriptures have been revealed. To this bear witness all created things.*"

Difference Between Bahá'í Faith and Ecclesiastical Organizations

5. It behooves us, dear friends, to endeavor not only to familiarize ourselves with the essential features of this supreme Handiwork of Bahá'u'lláh, but also to grasp the funda-

mental difference existing between this world-embracing, divinely-appointed Order and the chief ecclesiastical organizations of the world, whether they pertain to the Church of Christ, or to the ordinances of the Muḥammadan Dispensation.

For those whose priceless privilege is to guard over, administer the affairs, and advance the interests of these Bahá'í institutions will have, sooner or later, to face this searching question: "Where and how does this Order established by Bahá'u'lláh, which to outward seeming is but a replica of the institutions established in Christianity and Islám, differ from them? Are not the twin institutions of the House of Justice and of the Guardianship, the institution of the Hands of the Cause of God, the institution of the national and local Assemblies, the institution of the Mashriqu'l-Adhkár, but different names for the institutions of the Papacy and the Caliphate, with all their attending ecclesiastical orders which the Christians and Moslems uphold and advocate? What can possibly be the agency that can safeguard these Bahá'í institutions, so strikingly resemblant, in some of their features, to those which have been reared by the Fathers of the Church and the Apostles of Muḥammad, from witnessing the deterioration in character, the breach of unity, and the extinction of influence, which have befallen all organized religious hierarchies? Why should they not eventually suffer the selfsame fate that has overtaken the institutions which the successors of Christ and Muḥammad have reared?"

Upon the answer given to these challenging questions will, in a great measure, depend the success of the efforts which believers in every land are now exerting for the establishment of God's kingdom upon the earth. Few will fail to recognize that the Spirit breathed by Bahá'u'lláh upon the world, and which is manifesting itself with varying degrees of intensity through the efforts consciously displayed by His avowed supporters and indirectly through certain humanitarian organizations, can never permeate and exercise an abiding influence upon mankind unless and until it incarnates itself in a visible Order, which would bear His name, wholly identify itself with His principles, and function in conformity with His laws. That Bahá'u'lláh in His Book of Aqdas, and later 'Abdu'l-Bahá in His Will—a document which confirms, supplements, and correlates the provisions of the Aqdas—have set forth in their entirety those essential elements for the constitution of the world Bahá'í Commonwealth, no one who has read them will deny. According to these divinely-ordained administrative principles, the Dispensation of Bahá'u'lláh—the Ark of human salvation—must needs be modeled. From them, all future blessings must flow, and upon them its inviolable authority must ultimately rest.

For Bahá'u'lláh, we should readily recognize, has not only imbued mankind with a new and regenerating Spirit. He has not merely enunciated certain universal principles, or propounded a particular philosophy, however potent, sound and universal these may be. In addition to these He, as well as 'Abdu'l-Bahá after Him, has, unlike the Dispensations of the past, clearly and specifically laid down a set of Laws, established definite institutions, and provided for the essentials of a Divine Economy. These are destined to be a pattern for future society, a supreme instrument for the establishment of the Most Great Peace, and the one agency for the unification of the world, and the proclamation of the reign of righteousness and justice upon the earth. Not only have They revealed all the directions required for the practical realization of those ideals which the Prophets of God have visualized, and which from time immemorial have inflamed the imagination of seers and poets in every age. They have also, in unequivocal and emphatic language, appointed those twin institutions of the House of Justice and of the Guardianship as their chosen Successors, destined to apply the principles, promulgate the laws, protect the institutions, adapt loyally and intelligently the Faith to the requirements of progressive society, and consummate the incorruptible inheritance which the Founders of the Faith have bequeathed to the world.

Should we look back upon the past, were we to search out

the Gospel and Qur'án, we will readily recognize that neither the Christian nor the Islamic Dispensations can offer a parallel either to the system of Divine Economy so thoroughly established by Bahá'u'lláh, or to the safeguards which He has provided for its preservation and advancement. Therein, I am profoundly convinced, lies the answer to those questions to which I have already referred.

None, I feel, will question the fact that the fundamental reason why the unity of the Church of Christ was irretrievably shattered, and its influence was in the course of time undermined, was that the Edifice which the Fathers of the Church reared after the passing of His First Apostle was an Edifice that rested in nowise upon the explicit directions of Christ Himself. The authority and features of their administration were wholly inferred, and indirectly derived, with more or less justification, from certain vague and fragmentary references which they found scattered amongst His utterances as recorded in the Gospel. Not one of the sacraments of the Church; not one of the rites and ceremonies which the Christian Fathers have elaborately devised and ostentatiously observed; not one of the elements of the severe discipline they rigorously imposed upon the primitive Christians; none of these reposed on the direct authority of Christ, or emanated from His specific utterances. Not one of these did Christ conceive, none did He specifically invest with sufficient authority to either interpret His Word, or to add to what He had not specifically enjoined.

For this reason, in later generations, voices were raised in protest against the self-appointed Authority which arrogated to itself privileges and powers which did not emanate from the clear text of the Gospel of Jesus Christ, and which constituted a grave departure from the spirit which that Gospel did inculcate. They argued with force and justification that the canons promulgated by the Councils of the Church were not divinely-appointed laws, but were merely human devices which did not even rest upon the actual utterances of

Jesus. Their contention centered around the fact that the vague and inconclusive words, addressed by Christ to Peter, "Thou art Peter, and upon this rock I will build my Church," could never justify the extreme measures, the elaborate ceremonials, the fettering creeds and dogmas, with which His successors have gradually burdened and obscured His Faith. Had it been possible for the Church Fathers, whose unwarranted authority was thus fiercely assailed from every side, to refute the denunciations heaped upon them by quoting specific utterances of Christ regarding the future administration of His Church, or the nature of the authority of His Successors, they would surely have been capable of quenching the flame of controversy, and preserving the unity of Christendom. The Gospel, however, the only repository of the utterances of Christ, afforded no such shelter to these harassed leaders of the Church, who found themselves helpless in the face of the pitiless onslaught of their enemy, and who eventually had to submit to the forces of schism which invaded their ranks.

In the Muḥammadan Revelation, however, although His Faith as compared with that of Christ was, so far as the administration of His Dispensation is concerned, more complete and more specific in its provisions, yet in the matter of succession, it gave no written, no binding and conclusive instructions to those whose mission was to propagate His Cause. For the text of the Qur'án, the ordinances of which regarding prayer, fasting, marriage, divorce, inheritance, pilgrimage, and the like, have after the revolution of thirteen hundred years remained intact and operative, gives no definite guidance regarding the Law of Succession, the source of all the dissensions, the controversies, and schisms which have dismembered and discredited Islám.

Not so with the Revelation of Bahá'u'lláh. Unlike the Dispensation of Christ, unlike the Dispensation of Muḥammad, unlike all the Dispensations of the past, the apostles of Bahá'u'lláh in every land, wherever they labor and toil, have before them in clear, in unequivocal and emphatic language, all the laws, the regulations, the principles, the institutions, the guidance, they require for the prosecution and consummation of their task. Both in the administrative provisions of the Bahá'í Dispensation, and in the matter of succession, as embodied in the twin institutions of the House of Justice and of the Guardianship, the followers of Bahá'u'lláh can summon to their aid such irrefutable evidences of Divine Guidance that none can resist, that none can belittle or ignore. Therein lies the distinguishing feature of the Bahá'í Revelation. Therein lies the strength of the unity of the Faith, of the validity of a Revelation that claims not to destroy or belittle previous Revelations, but to connect, unify, and fulfill them. This is the reason why Bahá'u'lláh and 'Abdu'l-Bahá have both revealed and even insisted upon certain details in connection with the Divine Economy which they have bequeathed to us, their followers. This is why such an emphasis has been placed in their Will and Testament upon the powers and prerogatives of the ministers of their Faith.

The Vehicle of Revelation

6. Let no one meditating . . . on the nature of the Revelation of Bahá'u'lláh, mistake its character or misconstrue the intent of its Author. The divinity attributed to so great a Being and the complete incarnation of the names and attributes of God in so exalted a Person should, under no circumstances, be misconceived or misinterpreted. The human temple that has been made the vehicle of so overpowering a Revelation must, if we be faithful to the tenets of our Faith, ever remain entirely distinguished from that "innermost Spirit of Spirits" and "eternal Essence of Essences"—that invisible yet rational God Who, however much we extol the divinity of His Manifestations on earth, can in no wise incarnate His infinite, His unknowable, His incorruptible and all-embracing Reality in the concrete and limited frame of a

mortal being. Indeed, the God Who could so incarnate His own reality would, in the light of the teachings of Bahá'u'lláh, cease immediately to be God. So crude and fantastic a theory of Divine incarnation is as removed from, and incompatible with, the essentials of Bahá'í belief as are the no less inadmissible pantheistic and anthropomorphic conceptions of God—both of which the utterances of Bahá'u'lláh emphatically repudiate and the fallacy of which they expose.

The Báb

7. That the Báb, the inaugurator of the Bábí Dispensation, is fully entitled to rank as one of the self-sufficient Manifestions of God, that He has been invested with sovereign power and authority, and exercises all the rights and prerogatives of independent Prophethood, is yet another fundamental verity which the Message of Bahá'u'lláh insistently proclaims and which its followers must uncompromisingly uphold. That He is not to be regarded merely as an inspired Precursor of the Bahá'í Revelation, that in His person, as He Himself bears witness in the Persian Bayán, the object of all the Prophets gone before Him has been fulfilled, is a truth which I feel it my duty to demonstrate and emphasize. . . .

There can be no doubt that the claim to the twofold station ordained for the Báb by the Almighty, a claim which He Himself has so boldly advanced, which Bahá'u'lláh has repeatedly affirmed, and to which the Will and Testament of 'Abdu'l-Bahá has finally given the sanction of its testimony, constitutes the most distinctive feature of the Bahá'í Dispensation. It is a further evidence of its uniqueness, a tremendous accession to the strength, to the mysterious power and authority with which this holy cycle has been invested. Indeed the greatness of the Báb consists primarily, not in His being the divinely-appointed Forerunner of so transcendent a Revelation, but rather in His having been invested with the powers inherent in the inaugurator of a separate religious Dispensation, and in His wielding, to a degree unrivaled by the Messengers gone before Him, the scepter of independent Prophethood.

The short duration of His Dispensation, the restricted range within which His laws and ordinances have been made to operate, supply no criterion whatever wherewith to judge its Divine origin and to evaluate the potency of its message. *"That so brief a span,"* Bahá'u'lláh Himself explains, *"should have separated this most mighty and wondrous Revelation from Mine own previous Manifestation, is a secret that no man can unravel and a mystery such as no mind can fathom. Its duration had been foreordained, and no man shall ever discover its reason unless and until he be informed of the contents of My Hidden Book."* *"Behold,"* Bahá'u'lláh further explains in the Kitáb-i-Badí', one of His works refuting the arguments of the people of the Bayán, *"behold, how immediately upon the completion of the ninth year of this wondrous, this most holy and merciful Dispensation, the requisite number of pure, of wholly consecrated and sanctified souls had been most secretly consummated."*

'Abdu'l-Bahá

8. An attempt I strongly feel should now be made to clarify our minds regarding the station occupied by 'Abdu'l-Bahá and the significance of His position in this holy Dispensation. It would be indeed difficult for us, who stand so close to such a tremendous figure and are drawn by the mysterious power of so magnetic a personality, to obtain a clear and exact understanding of the rôle and character of One Who, not only in the Dispensation of Bahá'u'lláh but in the entire field of religious history, fulfills a unique function. Though moving in a sphere of His own and holding a rank radically different from that of the Author and the Forerunner of the Bahá'í Revelation, He, by virtue of the station ordained for Him through the Covenant of Bahá'u'lláh, forms together with them what may be termed the Three Central Figures of a Faith that stands unapproached in the world's spiritual his-

tory. He towers, in conjunction with them, above the destinies of this infant Faith of God from a level to which no individual or body ministering to its needs after Him, and for no less a period than a full thousand years, can ever hope to rise. To degrade His lofty rank by indentifying His station with or by regarding it as roughly equivalent to, the position of those on whom the mantle of His authority has fallen would be an act of impiety as grave as the no less heretical belief that inclines to exalt Him to a state of absolute equality with either the central Figure or Forerunner of our Faith. For wide as is the gulf that separates 'Abdu'l-Bahá from Him Who is the Source of an independent Revelation, it can never be regarded as commensurate with the greater distance that stands between Him Who is the Center of the Covenant and His ministers who are to carry on His work, whatever be their name, their rank, their functions or their future achievements. Let those who have known 'Abdu'l-Bahá, who through their contact with His magnetic personality have come to cherish for Him so fervent an admiration, reflect, in the light of this statement, on the greatness of One Who is so far above Him in station.

That 'Abdu'l-Bahá is not a Manifestation of God, that, though the successor of His Father, He does not occupy a cognate station, that no one else except the Báb and Bahá'u'lláh can ever lay claim to such a station before the expiration of a full thousand years—are verities which lie embedded in the specific utterances of both the Founder of our Faith and the Interpreter of His teachings. . . .

He is, and should for all time be regarded, first and foremost, as the Center and Pivot of Bahá'u'lláh's peerless and all-enfolding Covenant, His most exalted handiwork, the stainless Mirror of His light, the perfect Exemplar of His teachings, the unerring Interpreter of His Word, the embodiment of every Bahá'í ideal, the incarnation of every Bahá'í virtue, the Most Mighty Branch sprung from the Ancient Root, the Limb of the Law of God, the Being "*round Whom all names revolve,*" the Mainspring of the Oneness of Humanity, the Ensign of the Most Great Peace, the Moon of the Central Orb of this most holy Dispensation—styles and titles that are implicit and find their truest, their highest and fairest expression in the magic name 'Abdu'l-Bahá. He is, above and beyond these appellations, the *"Mystery of God"*—an expression by which Bahá'u'lláh Himself has chosen to designate Him, and which, while it does not by any means justify us to assign to Him the station of Prophethood, indicates how in the person of 'Abdu'l-Bahá the incompatible characteristics of a human nature and superhuman knowledge and perfection have been blended and are completely harmonized. . . .

That 'Abdu'l-Bahá is not a Manifestation of God, that He gets His light, His inspiration and sustenance direct from the Fountainhead of the Bahá'í Revelation; that He reflects even as a clear and perfect Mirror the rays of Bahá'u'lláh's glory, and does not inherently possess that indefinable yet all-pervading reality the exclusive possession of which is the hallmark of Prophethood; that His words are not equal in rank, though they possess an equal validity with the utterances of Bahá'u'lláh; that He is not to be acclaimed as the return of Jesus Christ, the Son Who will come "in the glory of the Father"—these truths find added justification, and are further reinforced, by the following statement of 'Abdu'l-Bahá, addressed to some believers in America, with which I may well conclude this section: *"You have written that there is a difference among the believers concerning the 'Second Coming of Christ.' Gracious God! Time and again this question hath arisen, and its answer hath emanated in a clear and irrefutable statement from the pen of 'Abdu'l-Bahá, that what is meant in the prophecies by the 'Lord of Hosts' and the 'Promised Christ' is the Blessed Perfection* (Bahá'u'lláh) *and His holiness the Exalted One* (the Báb). *My name is 'Abdu'l-Bahá. My qualification is 'Abdu'l-Bahá. My reality is 'Abdu'l-Bahá. My praise is 'Abdu'l-Bahá. Thraldom to the Blessed Perfection is my glorious and refulgent diadem, and servitude to all the human race my perpetual religion . . . No name, no title, no mention, no commendation have I, nor will ever have, except 'Abdu'l-Bahá. This is my longing. This is my greatest yearning. This is my eternal life. This is my everlasting glory.''*

'Abdu'l-Bahá's Testament

9. With the ascension of Bahá'u'lláh the Day-Star of Divine guidance which, as foretold by Shaykh Aḥmad and Siyyid Kázim, had risen in Shíráz, and, while pursuing its westward course, had mounted its zenith in Adrianople, had finally sunk below the horizon of 'Akká, never to rise again ere the complete revolution of one thousand years. The setting of so effulgent an Orb brought to a definite termination the period of Divine Revelation—the initial and most vitalizing stage in the Bahá'í era. Inaugurated by the Báb, culminating in Bahá'u'lláh, anticipated and extolled by the entire company of the Prophets of this great prophetic cycle, this period has, except for the short interval between the Báb's martyrdom and Bahá'u'lláh's shaking experiences in the Síyáh-Chál of Ṭihrán, been characterized by almost fifty years of continuous and progressive Revelation—a period which by its duration and fecundity must be regarded as unparalleled in the entire field of the world's spiritual history.

The passing of 'Abdu'l-Bahá, on the other hand, marks the closing of the Heroic and Apostolic Age of this same Dispensation—that primitive period of our Faith the splendors of which can never be rivaled, much less be eclipsed, by the magnificence that must needs distinguish the future victories of Bahá'u'lláh's Revelation. For neither the achievements of the champion-builders of the present-day institutions of the Faith of Bahá'u'lláh, nor the tumultuous triumphs which the heroes of its Golden Age will in the coming days succeed in winning, can measure with, or be included within the same category as, the wondrous works associated with the names of those who have generated its very life and laid its pristine foundations. That first and creative age of the Bahá'í era must, by its very nature, stand above and apart from the formative period into which we have entered and the golden age destined to succeed it.

'Abdu'l-Bahá, Who incarnates an institution for which we can find no parallel whatsoever in any of the world's recognized religious systems, may be said to have closed the Age to which He Himself belonged and opened the one in which we are now laboring. His Will and Testament should thus be regarded as the perpetual, the indissoluble link which the mind of Him Who is the Mystery of God has conceived in order to insure the continuity of the three ages that constitute the component parts of the Bahá'í Dispensation. The period in which the seed of the Faith had been slowly germinating is thus intertwined both with the one which must witness its efflorescence and the subsequent age in which that seed will have finally yielded its golden fruit.

The creative energies released by the Law of Bahá'u'lláh, permeating and evolving within the mind of 'Abdu'l-Bahá, have, by their very impact and close interaction, given birth to an Instrument which may be viewed as the Charter of the New World Order which is at once the glory and the promise of this most great Dispensation. The Will may thus be acclaimed as the inevitable offspring resulting from that mystic intercourse between Him Who communicated the generating influence of His divine Purpose and the One Who was its vehicle and chosen recipient. Being the Child of the Covenant—the Heir of both the Originator and the Interpreter of the Law of God—the Will and Testament of 'Abdu'l-Bahá can no more be divorced from Him Who supplied the original and motivating impulse than from the One Who ultimately conceived it. Bahá'u'lláh's inscrutable purpose, we must ever bear in mind, has been so thoroughly infused into the conduct of 'Abdu'l-Bahá, and their motives have been so closely wedded together, that the mere attempt to dissociate the teachings of the former from any system which the ideal

Exemplar of those same teachings has established would amount to a repudiation of one of the most sacred and basic truths of the Faith. . . .

It should be noted in this connection that this Administrative Order is fundamentally different from anything that any Prophet has previously established, inasmuch as Bahá'u'lláh has Himself revealed its principles, established its institutions, appointed the person to interpret His Word and conferred the necessary authority on the body designed to supplement and apply His legislative ordinances. Therein lies the secret of its strength, its fundamental distinction, and the guarantee against disintegration and schism. Nowhere in the sacred scriptures of any of the world's religious systems, nor even in the writings of the Inaugurator of the Bábí Dispensation, do we find any provisions establishing a covenant or providing for an administrative order that can compare in scope and authority with those that lie at the very basis of the Bahá'í Dispensation. Has either Christianity or Islám, to take as an instance two of the most widely diffused and outstanding among the world's recognized religions, anything to offer that can measure with, or be regarded as equivalent to, either the Book of Bahá'u'lláh's Covenant or to the Will and Testament of 'Abdu'l-Bahá? Does the text of either the Gospel or the Qur'án confer sufficient authority upon those leaders and councils that have claimed the right and assumed the function of interpreting the provisions of their sacred scriptures and of administering the affairs of their respective communities? Could Peter, the admitted chief of the Apostles, or the Imám 'Alí, the cousin and legitimate successor of the Prophet, produce in support of the primacy with which both had been invested written and explicit affirmations from Christ and Muḥammad that could have silenced those who either among their contemporaries or in a later age have repudiated their authority and, by their action, precipitated the schisms that persist until the present day? Where, we may confidently ask, in the recorded sayings of Jesus Christ, whether in the matter of succession or in the provision of a set of specific laws and clearly defined administrative ordinances, as distinguished from purely spiritual principles, can we find anything approaching the detailed injunctions, laws and warnings that abound in the authenticated utterances of both Bahá'u'lláh and 'Abdu'l-Bahá? Can any passage of the Qur'án, which in respect to its legal code, its administrative and devotional ordinances marks already a notable advance over previous and more corrupted Revelations, be construed as placing upon an unassailable basis the undoubted authority with which Muhammad had, verbally and on several occasions, invested His successor? Can the Author of the Bábí Dispensation however much He may have succeeded through the provisions of the Persian Bayán in averting a schism as permanent and catastrophic as those that afflicted Christianity and Islám—can He be said to have produced instruments for the safeguarding of His Faith as definite and efficacious as those which must for all time preserve the unity of the organized followers of the Faith of Bahá'u'lláh?

Alone of all the Revelations gone before it this Faith has, through the explicit directions, the repeated warnings, the authenticated safeguards incorporated and elaborated in its teachings, succeeded in raising a structure which the bewildered followers of bankrupt and broken creeds might well approach and critically examine, and seek, ere it is too late, the invulnerable security of its world-embracing shelter.

The Divine Program

10. Humanity, whether viewed in the light of man's individual conduct or in the existing relationships between organized communities and nations, has, alas, strayed too far and suffered too great a decline to be redeemed through the unaided efforts of the best among its recognized rulers and statesmen—however disinterested their motives, however concerted their action, however unsparing in their zeal and

devotion to its cause. No scheme which the calculations of the highest statesmanship may yet devise; no doctrine which the most distinguished exponents of economic theory may hope to advance; no principle which the most ardent of moralists may strive to inculcate, can provide, in the last resort, adequate foundations upon which the future of a distracted world can be built. No appeal for mutual tolerance which the worldly-wise might raise, however compelling and insistent, can calm its passions or help restore its vigor. Nor would any general scheme of mere organized international coöperation, in whatever sphere of human activity, however ingenious in conception, or extensive in scope, succeed in removing the root cause of the evil that has so rudely upset the equilibrium of present-day society. Not even, I venture to assert, would the very act of devising the machinery required for the political and economic unification of the world—a principle that has been increasingly advocated in recent times—provide in itself the antidote against the poison that is steadily undermining the vigor of organized peoples and nations. What else, might we not confidently affirm, but the unreserved acceptance of the Divine Program enunciated, with such simplicity and force . . . , by Bahá'u'lláh, embodying in its essentials God's divinely appointed scheme for the unification of mankind in this age, coupled with an indomitable conviction in the unfailing efficacy of each and all of its provisions, is eventually capable of withstanding the forces of internal disintegration which, if unchecked, must needs continue to eat into the vitals of a despairing society. It is towards this goal—the goal of a new World Order, Divine in origin, all-embracing in scope, equitable in principle, challenging in its features—that a harassed humanity must strive.

11. How pathetic indeed are the efforts of those leaders of human institutions who, in utter disregard of the spirit of the age, are striving to adjust national processes, suited to the

ancient days of self-contained nations, to an age which must either achieve the unity of the world, as adumbrated by Bahá'u'lláh, or perish. At so critical an hour in the history of civilization it behooves the leaders of all the nations of the world, great and small, whether in the East or in the West, whether victors or vanquished, to give heed to the clarion call of Bahá'u'lláh and, thoroughly imbued with a sense of world solidarity, the *sine quâ non* of loyalty to His Cause, arise manfully to carry out in its entirety the one remedial scheme He, the Divine Physician, has prescribed for an ailing humanity. Let them discard, once for all, every preconceived idea, every national prejudice, and give heed to the sublime counsel of 'Abdu'l-Bahá, the authorized Expounder of His teachings. You can best serve your country, was 'Abdu'l-Bahá's rejoinder to a high official in the service of the federal government of the United States of America, who had questioned Him as to the best manner in which he could promote the interests of his government and people, if you strive, in your capacity as a citizen of the world, to assist in the eventual application of the principle of federalism underlying the government of your own country to the relationships now existing between the peoples and nations of the world.

12. Surely the world, contracted and transformed into a single highly complex organism by the marvellous progress achieved in the realm of physical science, by the world-wide expansion of commerce and industry, and struggling, under the pressure of world economic forces, amidst the pitfalls of a materialistic civilzation, stands in dire need of a restatement of the Truth underlying all the Revelation of the past in a language suited to its essential requirements. And what voice other than that of Bahá'u'lláh—the Mouthpiece of God for this age—is capable of effecting a transformation of society as radical as that which He has already accomplished in the hearts of those men and women, so diversified and seemingly

irreconcilable, who constitute the body of His declared followers throughout the world?

This New World Order

13. This New World Order, whose promise is enshrined in the Revelation of Bahá'u'lláh, whose fundamental principles have been enunciated in the writings of the Center of His Covenant, involves no less than the complete unification of the entire human race. This unification should conform to such principles as would directly harmonize with the spirit that animates, and the laws that govern the operation of, the institutions that already constitute the structural basis of the Administrative Order of His Faith.

No machinery falling short of the standard inculcated by the Bahá'í Revelation, and at variance with the sublime pattern ordained in His teachings, which the collective efforts of mankind may yet devise can ever hope to achieve anything above or beyond that *"Lesser Peace"* to which the Author of our Faith has Himself alluded in His writings. *"Now that ye have refused the Most Great Peace,"* He, admonishing the kings and rulers of the earth, has written, *"hold ye fast unto this the Lesser Peace, that haply ye may in some degree better your own condition and that of your dependents."* Expatiating on this Lesser Peace, He thus addresses in that same Tablet the rulers of the earth: *"Be reconciled among yourselves, that ye may need no more armaments save in a measure to safeguard your territories and dominions . . . Be united, O kings of the earth, for thereby will the tempest of discord be stilled amongst you, and your peoples find rest, if ye be of them that comprehend. Should any one among you take up arms against another, rise ye all against him, for this is naught but manifest justice."*

The Most Great Peace, on the other hand, as conceived by Bahá'u'lláh—a peace that must inevitably follow as the practical consequence of the spiritualization of the world and the fusion of all its races, creeds, classes and nations—can rest on no other basis, and can be preserved through no other agency, except the divinely appointed ordinances that are implicit in the World Order that stands associated with His Holy Name. In His Tablet, revealed almost seventy years ago to Queen Victoria, Bahá'u'lláh, alluding to this Most Great Peace, has declared: *"That which the Lord hath ordained as the sovereign remedy and mightiest instrument for the healing of all the world is the union of all its peoples in one universal Cause, one common Faith. This can in no wise be achieved except through the power of a skilled, an all-powerful and inspired Physician. This, verily, is the truth, and all else naught but error . . . Consider these days in which the Ancient Beauty, He Who is the Most Great Name, hath been sent down to regenerate and unify mankind. Behold how with drawn swords they rose against Him, and committed that which caused the Faithful Spirit to tremble. And whenever We said unto them: 'Lo, the World Reformer is come,' they made reply: 'He, in truth, is one of the stirrers of mischief.'"* "It beseemeth all men in this Day," He, in another Tablet, asserts, *"to take firm hold on the Most Great Name, and to establish the unity of all mankind. There is no place to flee to, no refuge that any one can seek, except Him."*

The Revelation of Bahá'u'lláh, whose supreme mission is none other but the achievement of this organic and spiritual unity of the whole body of nations, should, if we be faithful to its implications, be regarded as signalizing through its advent the *coming of age of the entire human race*. It should be viewed not merely as yet another spiritual revival in the ever-changing fortunes of mankind, not only as a further stage in a chain of progressive Revelations, nor even as the culmination of one of a series of recurrent prophetic cycles, but rather as marking the last and highest stage in the stupendous evolution of man's collective life on this planet.

The emergence of a world community, the consciousness of world citizenship, the founding of a world civilization and culture—all of which must synchronize with the initial stages in the unfoldment of the Golden Age of the Bahá'í Era —should, by their very nature, be regarded, as far as this planetary life is concerned, as the furthermost limits in the organization of human society, though man, as an individual, will, nay must indeed as a result of such a consummation, continue indefinitely to progress and develop.

That mystic, all-pervasive, yet indefinable change, which we associate with the stage of maturity inevitable in the life of the individual and development of the fruit must, if we would correctly apprehend the utterances of Bahá'u'lláh, have its counterpart in the evolution of the organization of human society. A similar stage must sooner or later be attained in the collective life of mankind, producing an even more striking phenomenon in world relations, and endowing the whole human race with such potentialities of well-being as shall provide, throughout the succeeding ages, the chief incentive required for the eventual fulfillment of its high destiny. Such a stage of maturity in the process of human government must, for all time, if we would faithfully recognize the tremendous claim advanced by Bahá'u'lláh, remain identified with the Revelation of which He was the Bearer.

14. Let no one, while this System is still in its infancy, misconceive its character, belittle its significance or misrepresent its purpose. The bedrock on which this Administrative Order is founded is God's immutable Purpose for mankind in this day. The Source from which it derives its inspiration is no one less than Bahá'u'lláh Himself. Its shield and defender are the embattled hosts of the Abhá Kingdom. Its seed is the blood of no less than twenty thousand martyrs who have offered up their lives that it may be born and flourish. The axis round which its institutions revolve are the authentic provisions of the Will and Testament of 'Abdu'l-Bahá. Its

guiding principles are the truths which He Who is the unerring Interpreter of the teachings of our Faith has so clearly
enunciated in His public addresses throughout the West. The
laws that govern its operation and limit its functions are
those which have been expressly ordained in the Kitáb-i-
Aqdas. The seat round which its spiritual, its humanitarian
and administrative activities will cluster are the
Mashriqu'l-Adhkár and its Dependencies. The pillars that
sustain its authority and buttress its structure are the twin institutions of the Guardianship and of the Universal House of
Justice. The central, the underlying aim which animates it is
the establishment of the New World Order as adumbrated by
Bahá'u'lláh. The methods it employs, the standard it inculcates, incline it to neither East nor West, neither Jew nor
Gentile, neither rich nor poor, neither white nor colored. Its
watchword is the unification of the human race; its standard
the "Most Great Peace"; its consummation the advent of that
golden millennium—the Day when the kingdoms of this
world shall have become the Kingdom of God Himself, the
Kingdom of Bahá'u'lláh.

The Principle of Oneness

15. Let there be no misgivings as to the animating purpose of
the world-wide Law of Bahá'u'lláh. Far from aiming at the
subversion of the existing foundations of society, it seeks to
broaden its basis, to remold its institutions in a manner
consonant with the needs of an ever-changing world. It can
conflict with no legitimate allegiances, nor can it undermine
essential loyalties. Its purpose is neither to stifle the flame
of a sane and intelligent patriotism in men's hearts, nor to
abolish the system of national autonomy so essential if the
evils of excessive centralization are to be avoided. It does not
ignore, nor does it attempt to suppress, the diversity of
ethnical origins, of climate, of history, of language and
tradition, of thought and habit, that differentiate the peoples

and nations of the world. It calls for a wider loyalty, for a larger aspiration than any that has animated the human race. It insists upon the subordination of national impulses and interests to the imperative claims of a unified world. It repudiates excessive centralization on one hand, and disclaims all attempts at uniformity on the other. Its watchword is unity in diversity such as 'Abdu'l-Bahá Himself has explained:

"Consider the flowers of a garden. Though differing in kind, color, form and shape, yet, inasmuch as they are refreshed by the waters of one spring, revived by the breath of one wind, invigorated by the rays of one sun, this diversity increaseth their charm and addeth unto their beauty. How unpleasing to the eye if all the flowers and plants, the leaves and blossoms, the fruit, the branches and the trees of that garden were all of the same shape and color! Diversity of hues, form and shape enricheth and adorneth the garden, and heighteneth the effect thereof. In like manner, when divers shades of thought, temperament and character, are brought together under the power and influence of one central agency, the beauty and glory of human perfection will be revealed and made manifest. Naught but the celestial potency of the Word of God, which ruleth and transcendeth the realities of all things, is capable of harmonizing the divergent thoughts, sentiments, ideas and convictions of the children of men."

The call of Bahá'u'lláh is primarily directed against all forms of provincialism, all insularities and prejudices. If long-cherished ideals and time-honored institutions, if certain social assumptions and religious formulae have ceased to promote the welfare of the generality of mankind, if they no longer minister to the needs of a continually evolving humanity, let them be swept away and relegated to the limbo of obsolescent and forgotten doctrines. Why should these, in a world subject to the immutable law of change and decay, be exempt from the deterioration that must needs overtake every human institution? For legal standards, political and economic theories are solely designed to safeguard the interests of humanity as a whole, and not humanity to be crucified for the preservation of the integrity of any particular law or doctrine.

Let there be no mistake. The principle of the Oneness of Mankind—the pivot round which all the teachings of Bahá'u'lláh revolve—is no mere outburst of ignorant emotionalism or an expression of vague and pious hope. Its appeal is not to be merely identified with a reawakening of the spirit of brotherhood and good-will among men, nor does it aim solely at the fostering of harmonious coöperation among individual peoples and nations. Its implications are deeper, its claims greater than any which the Prophets of old were allowed to advance. Its message is applicable not only to the individual, but concerns itself primarily with the nature of those essential relationships that must bind all the states and nations and members of one human family. It does not constitute merely the enunciation of an ideal, but stands inseparably associated with an institution adequate to embody its truth, demonstrate its validity, and perpetuate its influence. It implies an organic change in the structure of present-day society, a change such as the world has not yet experienced. It constitutes a challenge, at once bold and universal, to outworn shibboleths of national creeds—creeds that have had their day and which must, in the ordinary course of events as shaped and controlled by Providence, give way to a new gospel, fundamentally different from, and infinitely superior to, what the world has already conceived. It calls for no less than the reconstruction and the demilitarization of the whole civilized world—a world organically unified in all the essential aspects of its life, its political machinery, its spiritual aspiration, its trade and finance, its script and language, and yet infinite in the diversity of the national characteristics of its federated units.

It represents the consummation of human evolution—an

evolution that has had its earliest beginnings in the birth of family life, its subsequent development in the achievement of tribal solidarity, leading in turn to the constitution of the city-state, and expanding later into the institution of independent and sovereign nations.

The principle of the Oneness of Mankind, as proclaimed by Bahá'u'lláh, carries with it no more and no less than a solemn assertion that attainment to this final stage in this stupendous evolution is not only necessary but inevitable, that its realization is fast approaching, and that nothing short of a power that is born of God can succeed in establishing it.

Suffering More Intense

16. Who knows that for so exalted a conception to take shape a suffering more intense than any it has yet experienced will have to be inflicted upon humanity? Could anything less than the fire of a civil war with all its violence and vicissitudes—a war that nearly rent the great American Republic—have welded the states, not only into a Union of independent units, but into a Nation, in spite of all the ethnic differences that characterized its component parts? That so fundamental a revolution, involving such far-reaching changes in the structure of society, can be achieved through the ordinary processes of diplomacy and education seems highly improbable. We have but to turn our gaze to humanity's blood-stained history to realize that nothing short of intense mental as well as physical agony has been able to precipitate those epoch-making changes that constitute the greatest landmarks in the history of human civilization.

The Goal of Human Evolution

17. Unification of the whole of mankind is the hall-mark of the stage which human society is now approaching. Unity of family, of tribe, of city-state, and nation have been succes-

sively attempted and fully established. World unity is the goal towards which a harassed humanity is striving. Nation-building has come to an end. The anarchy inherent in state sovereignty is moving towards a climax. A world, growing to maturity, must abandon this fetish, recognize the oneness and wholeness of human relationships, and establish once for all the machinery that can best incarnate this fundamental principle of its life. . . .

The unity of the human race, as envisaged by Bahá'u'lláh, implies the establishment of a world commonwealth in which all nations, races, creeds and classes are closely and permanently united, and in which the autonomy of its state members and the personal freedom and initiative of the individuals that compose them are definitely and completely safeguarded. This commonwealth must, as far as we can visualize it, consist of a world legislature, whose members will, as the trustees of the whole of mankind, ultimately control the entire resources of all the component nations, and will enact such laws as shall be required to regulate the life, satisfy the needs and adjust the relationships of all races and peoples. A world executive, backed by an international Force, will carry out the decisions arrived at, and apply the laws enacted by, this world legislature, and will safeguard the organic unity of the whole commonwealth. A world tribunal will adjudicate and deliver its compulsory and final verdict in all and any disputes that may arise between the various elements constituting this universal system. A mechanism of world inter-communication will be devised, embracing the whole planet, freed from national hindrances and restrictions, and functioning with marvellous swiftness and perfect regularity. A world metropolis will act as the nerve center of a world civilization, the focus towards which the unifying forces of life will converge and from which its energizing influences will radiate. A world language will either be invented or chosen from among the existing lan-guages and will be taught in the schools of all the federated nations as an auxiliary to their mother tongue. A world script, a world literature, a uniform and universal system of currency, of weights and measures, will simplify and facilitate intercourse and understanding among the nations and races of mankind. In such a world society, science and religion, the two most potent forces in human life, will be reconciled, will coöperate, and will harmoniously develop. The press will, under such a system, while giving full scope to the expression of the diversified views and convictions of mankind, cease to be mischievously manipulated by vested interests, whether private or public, and will be liberated from the influence of contending governments and peoples. The economic resources of the world will be organized, its sources of raw materials will be tapped and fully utilized, its markets will be coördinated and developed, and the distribution of its products will be equitably regulated.

National rivalries, hatreds, and intrigues will cease, and racial animosity and prejudice will be replaced by racial amity, understanding and coöperation. The causes of religious strife will be permanently removed, economic barriers and restrictions will be completely abolished, and the inordinate distinction between classes will be obliterated. Destitution on the one hand, and gross accumulation of ownership on the other, will disappear. The enormous energy dissipated and wasted on war, whether economic or political, will be consecrated to such ends as will extend the range of human inventions and technical development, to the increase of the productivity of mankind, to the extermination of disease, to the extension of scientific research, to the raising of the standard of physical health, to the sharpening and refinement of the human brain, to the exploitation of the unused and unsuspected resources of the planet, to the prolongation of human life, and to the furtherance of any other agency that can stimulate the intellectual, the moral, and spiritual life of the entire human race.

A world federal system, ruling the whole earth and exercising unchallengeable authority over its unimaginably vast resources, blending and embodying the ideals of both the East and the West, liberated from the curse of war and its miseries, and bent on the exploitation of all the available sources of energy on the surface of the planet, a system in which Force is made the servant of Justice, whose life is sustained by its universal recognition of one God and by its allegiance to one common Revelation—such is the goal towards which humanity, impelled by the unifying forces of life, is moving.

"*One of the great events,*" affirms 'Abdu'l-Bahá, "*which is to occur in the Day of the manifestation of that incomparable Branch is the hoisting of the Standard of God among all nations. By this is meant that all nations and kindreds will be gathered together under the shadow of this Divine Banner, which is no other than the Lordly Branch itself, and will become a single nation. Religious and sectarian antagonism, the hostility of races and peoples, and differences among nations, will be eliminated. All men will adhere to one religion, will have one common faith, will be blended into one race and become a single people. All will dwell in one common fatherland, which is the planet itself.*" "*Now, in the world of being,*" He has moreover explained, "*the Hand of Divine power hath firmly laid the foundations of this all-highest bounty, and this wondrous gift. Whatsoever is latent in the innermost of this holy Cycle shall gradually appear and be made manifest, for now is but the beginning of its growth, and the dayspring of the revelation of its signs. Ere the close of this century and of this age, it shall be made clear and evident how wondrous was that spring-tide, and how heavenly was that gift.*"

The Radiant Future

18. The flames which His Divine justice have kindled cleanse an unregenerate humanity, and fuse its discordant, its war-

ring elements as no other agency can cleanse or fuse them. It is not only a retributory and destructive fire, but a disciplinary and creative process, whose aim is the salvation, through unification, of the entire planet. . . .

God's purpose is none other than to usher in, in ways He alone can bring about, and the full significance of which He alone can fathom, the Great, the Golden Age of a long-divided, a long-afflicted humanity. Its present state, indeed even its immediate future, is dark, distressingly dark. Its distant future, however, is radiant, gloriously radiant—so radiant that no eye can visualize it.

"The winds of despair," writes Bahá'u'lláh, as He surveys the immediate destinies of mankind, *"are, alas, blowing from every direction, and the strife that divides and afflicts the human race is daily increasing. The signs of impending convulsions and chaos can now be discerned, inasmuch as the prevailing order appears to be lamentably defective."* *"Such shall be its plight,"* He, in another connection, has declared, *"that to disclose it now would not be meet and seemly."* *"These fruitless strifes,"* He, on the other hand, contemplating the future of mankind, has emphatically prophesied, in the course of His memorable interview with the Persian orientalist, Edward G. Browne, *"these ruinous wars shall pass away and the 'Most Great Peace' shall come. . . . These strifes and this bloodshed and discord must cease, and all men be as one kindred and one family."* *"Soon,"* He predicts, *"will the present-day order be rolled up, and a new one spread out in its stead."* *"After a time,"* He also has written, *"all the governments on earth will change. Oppression will envelop the world. And following a universal convulsion, the sun of justice will rise from the horizon of the unseen realm."*

19. Dearly-beloved friends! A rectitude of conduct which, in all its manifestations, offers a striking contrast to the deceitfulness and corruption that characterize the political life of

the nation and of the parties and factions that compose it; a holiness and chastity that are diametrically opposed to the moral laxity and licentiousness which defile the character of a not inconsiderable proportion of its citizens; and inter-racial fellowship completely purged from the curse of racial prejudice which stigmatizes the vast majority of its people—these are the weapons which the American believers can and must wield in their double crusade, first to regenerate the inward life of their own community, and next to assail the long-standing evils that have entrenched themselves in the life of their nation. The perfection of such weapons, the wise and effective utilization of every one of them, more than the furtherance of any particular plan, or the devising of any special scheme, or the accumulation of any amount of material resources, can prepare them for the time when the Hand of Destiny will have directed them to assist in creating and in bringing into operation that World Order which is now incubating within the world-wide administrative institutions of their Faith.

20. Let not, however, the invincible army of Bahá'u'lláh, who in the West, and at one of its potential storm-centers is to fight, in His name and for His sake, one of its fiercest and most glorious battles, be afraid of any criticism that might be directed against it. Let it not be deterred by any condemnation with which the tongue of the slanderer may seek to debase its motives. Let it not recoil before the threatening advance of the forces of fanaticism, of orthodoxy, of corruption, and of prejudice that may be leagued against it. The voice of criticism is a voice that indirectly reinforces the proclamation of its Cause. Unpopularity but serves to throw into greater relief the contrast between it and its adversaries; while ostracism is itself the magnetic power that must eventually win over to its camp the most vociferous and inveterate amongst its foes. Already in the land where the greatest battles of the Faith have been fought, and its most rapacious

enemies have lived, the march of events, the slow yet steady infiltration of its ideals, and the fulfillment of its prophecies, have resulted not only in disarming and in transforming the character of some of its most redoubtable enemies, but also in securing their firm and unreserved allegiance to its Founders. So complete a transformation, so startling a reversal of attitude, can only be effected if that chosen vehicle which is designed to carry the Message of Bahá'u'lláh to the hungry, the restless, and unshepherded multitudes is itself thoroughly cleansed from the defilements which it seeks to remove.

It is upon you, therefore, my best-beloved friends, that I wish to impress not only the urgency and imperative necessity of your holy task, but also the limitless possibilities which it possesses of raising to such an exalted level not only the life and activities of your own community, but the motives and standards that govern the relationships existing among the people to which you belong. Undismayed by the formidable nature of this task, you will, I am confident, meet as befits you the challenge of these times, so fraught with peril, so full of corruption, and yet so pregnant with the promise of a future so bright that no previous age in the annals of mankind can rival its glory.

21. Not ours, puny mortals that we are, to attempt, at so critical a stage in the long and checkered history of mankind, to arrive at a precise and satisfactory understanding of the steps which must successively lead a bleeding humanity, wretchedly oblivious of its God, and careless of Bahá'u'lláh, from its calvary to its ultimate resurrection. Not ours, the living witnesses of the all-subduing potency of His Faith, to question, for a moment, and however dark the misery that enshrouds the world, the ability of Bahá'u'lláh to forge, with the hammer of His Will, and through the fire of tribulation, upon the anvil of this travailing age, and in the particular shape His mind has envisioned, these scattered and mutually destructive fragments into which a perverse world has fallen,

into one single unit, solid and indivisible, able to execute His design for the children of men.

Ours rather the duty, however confused the scene, however dismal the present outlook, however circumscribed the resources we dispose of, to labor serenely, confidently and unremittingly to lend our share of assistance, in whichever way circumstances may enable us, to the operation of the forces which, as marshaled and directed by Bahá'u'lláh, are leading humanity out of the valley of misery and shame to the loftiest summits of power and glory.

List of References
Key

ADJ Shoghi Effendi. *The Advent of Divine Justice*. 3rd rev. ed. Wilmette, Ill.: Bahá'í Publishing Trust, 1969.

PDIC ————. *The Promised Day Is Come*. Rev. ed. Wilmette, Ill.: Bahá'í Publishing Trust, 1961.

WOB ————. *The World Order of Bahá'u'lláh*. Rev. ed. Wilmette, Ill.: Bahá'í Publishing Trust, 1955.

1. WOB xi-xiii (1938 ed.)
2. WOB 57-58
3. WOB 60-61
4. WOB 103-04
5. WOB 18-22
6. WOB 112-13
7. WOB 123-24
8. WOB 131-32, 134, 139
9. WOB 143-46
10. WOB 33-34
11. WOB 36-37
12. WOB 47
13. WOB 162-64
14. WOB 156-57
15. WOB 41-43
16. WOB 45
17. WOB 202, 203-05
18. PDIC 120-21
19. ADJ 34-35
20. ADJ 35-36
21. PDIC 129